How to Start a Business in

NIGERIA

The Ultimate Guide to Doing Business in Nigeria

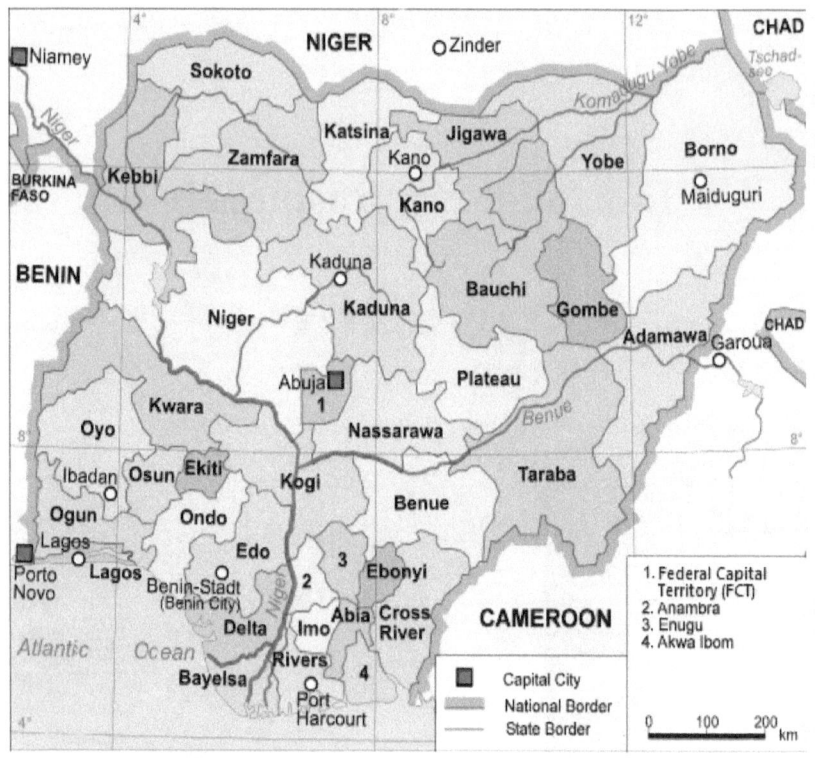

NIGER

CHAD

Niamey

Sokoto

Zinder

Kom Yobe

Tschad-
see

Katsina   Jigawa

Kano

Borno

BURKINA
FASO   Kebbi   Zamfara

Yobe

Kano   Maiduguri

BENIN

Kaduna

Bauchi

Gombe

CHAD

Niger   Kaduna

Adamawa   Garoua

Abuja   Plateau

Oyo   Kwara   Nassarawa   Benue

Ibadan   Osun   Ekiti   Kogi   Taraba

Ogun   Ondo   Benue

Lagos   Edo   Ebonyi

Porto   Lagos   Benin-Stadt   Abia   Cross   CAMEROON
Novo   (Benin City)   Delta   Imo   River

Atlantic   Ocean   Rivers

Bayelsa   Port
Harcourt

1. Federal Capital
Territory (FCT)
2. Anambra
3. Enugu
4. Akwa Ibom

Capital City
National Border
State Border

0   100   200
km

ii

Looking to Start a Business in Nigeria?

There are many reasons an entrepreneur or investor might be interested in the business prospects available in the country of Nigeria. The hardy economy, booming population, and untapped natural resources make it a prime candidate for helping grow new businesses.

Hardy Economy

The economy of Nigeria is relatively stable, even as the rest of the world is experiencing varying levels of recession. Nigeria is one of the top-ranking free market economies in all of Africa. A recent float of the Naira due to global recession, makes Nigeria a top candidate for foreign investments to pay off in higher-than-average rates.

Population Explosion

Nigeria is a land full of promises. Beyond the economic reasons, a second building block for opportunities and wealth, is its high rate of population expansion. Not only are more people being born in Nigeria, its population is largely under the age of 25, with a growing middle class (23% as of 2015). This results in more high-spending consumers and a broader customer base for all businesses.

As the people of Nigeria increase, so do the needs of the population as a whole; businesses meeting a specific need and ran with a well thought-out plan are almost guaranteed success in this most populous country in Africa.

Untapped Potential

Despite its reputation for being open to businesses and investments, it has a multitude of untapped opportunities for new organizations. Some of these opportunities are in the sectors of: Real Estate, Solid Minerals, Tourism, Power/energy, Regulatory Services, Security, Agriculture, Agribusiness, Automotive, ICT, Education and many more.

Why do business in Nigeria?

Nigeria is one of the largest countries in Africa, as well as the biggest African economy. It occupies a total geographical area of 923,768 square kilometers, with an estimated population of 197 million in 2018.

Today, Nigeria is one of the most attractive markets globally, with a GDP per capita of $2,177.99, in the year 2016 according to World bank. This is due to its abundant natural resources, favorable weather and climates, cost effective workforce (60% youth), strategic location in the West-African region, and high return on investment rate (35% - 45%).

With all of these factors and more, Nigeria is termed the "business hub of Africa".

Contents

CHAPTER 1
OVERVIEW OF NIGERIA FOR ENTREPRENEURS

General presentation

Nigeria, officially referred to as the Federal Republic of Nigeria, is a country located in West Africa. The country is known as Africa's most populated nation with FCT Abuja as the capital city. Built in the 1980s, Abuja is one of the most well planned city in the country. It was commissioned to replace Lagos as the capital of Nigeria in December 12, 1991. The city is the headquarters of many organisations and establishments in the nation, as it houses the Presidential Villa, National Assembly, Defence Head Quarters, and other Federal Ministries and Government Parastatals.

Lagos is the nation's commercial city and one of the largest cities in the country covering an area of 385.9 square miles. It is the most populous city in Africa with an estimated population of 21 million. The state is currently one of the fastest growing cities in Africa and also houses one of the largest and busiest ports on the continent, Port of Lagos (Apapa).

Another top commercial city in Nigeria is Kano. The city has a market with the highest amount of raw cash in circulation, compared to every other city.

Nigeria is covering a total area of 356,667 square miles. It is considered the seventh-most populous country in the world, with an estimated population of 182 million.

Nigeria is a country of rich ethnic diversity, composed of over 250 ethnic groups. The three largest ethnic groups in Nigeria are the Hausas (Northern), Igbos (Eastern) and Yorubas (Western). The other major tribes in the country include Edo, Ijaw, Kanuri, Ibibio, Ebira, Nupe and Tiv.

The government of Nigeria is a presidential federal republic: Current President - Muhammadu Buhari, and Vice President - Yemi Osinbajo. 29th May 2015 – (as of the production of this book in Oct 2018)

The Naira denoted by the ISO 4217 code NGN, as the nation's official currency, with English as the country's official language, which is extensively used for day to day communication across the country. Other indigenous languages such as Hausa, Yoruba and Igbo are also spoken by the majority of the citizens. A derived language called the *'Pidgin' or 'Broken English'* is also a popular lingua-franca in the country.

Nigeria is multi-religious, with majority of the population practicing either Christianity or Islam. The other minority religions in the country include Hinduism, Judaism, the Baha'i Faith, and Chrislam.

Nigeria often moves between the first or second positions as the largest economy in Africa. It is classified as an emerging market owing to its rich reserves of natural resources, and well-developed financial and communications sectors. The Nigerian Stock Exchange is the second-largest in Africa. Sighted by the NNPC (Nigerian National Petroleum Corporation), Nigeria is the sixth-largest producer of crude-oil in the world and its petroleum products significantly contribute to the nation's GDP. Other manufactured products such as leather, textiles, t-shirts, plastics and processed food, also contribute to the growth of the country's economy. However, agriculture is most important, as almost forty percent of Nigerians are engaged in the sector. Cocoa, Sugar cane, Yams, Maize, Palm oil, Groundnuts, Coconuts, Citrus fruits, Pearl millet, and Cassava are the major agricultural products.

That being said, health care and general living conditions in Nigeria are still relatively poor, and these pose a threat to the otherwise advancing country.

Nigeria's Local Culture and Climate

The nation is made up of over 250 ethnic groups, speaking over 250 languages and a multitude of dialects. It is divided into two major religious groups, Christianity and Islam. Christianity dominates the South, while Islam is predominantly practiced in the North.

Multicultural Nigeria is known over the world for its people's unique style of clothing. Despite cheaper, Western-influenced wear in the Southern parts of Nigeria, the common clothing for most Nigerians still remains the Buba style: a loose-fitting shirt and Fila (cap) for men. For women, a fitting blouse that falls beyond the waist and Gele (headgear). Women are also known to wear long, flowing robes and headscarves that are distinctively Nigerian.

This common Nigerian style of dressing is influenced partly by the climate, which is divided into four parts: tropical monsoon, tropical savanna, sahel, and alpine. The South Atlantic Ocean brings tropical monsoon weather to South Nigeria, while the Western and Central parts of Nigeria experience a tropical savanna climate. The North has less rainfall, which influences its Sahel climate.

Setting up a business in Nigeria can be a lucrative and fulfilling endeavor, if done with forethought and planning based on knowledge of the country, as it relates to its own culture and the rest of the world. Understanding the facts about Nigeria's structure, government, culture and economy, and how they affect the way businesses must be conducted, is the first step to starting a successful business in this West African country.

Giant of Africa

The Federal Republic of Nigeria carries the title "Giant of Africa", due to its massive population and growing economy. With an estimated 197 million citizens and over 923,768 (sq. km) surface area, it has the biggest population out of any African country, and is now the 30th largest economy in the world as of 2017.

According to the World Bank (2018), Nigeria now holds the 145th spot out of 190 economies in the ease of conducting business index. The report indicated that Nigeria had moved up 24 spots from the previous year after conducting various reforms to improve their business environment.

CHAPTER 2

THRIVING SECTORS FOR INVESTMENTS AND BUSINESS OPPORTUNITIES

Nigeria has many industries ripe for investment, but you will need to have an idea of which sectors are the best fit for your particular skillset. The most prominent sectors that offer opportunities for businesses and investments will be discussed in this chapter.

The Oil and Gas Industry

The latest report by the NNPC 2018 (Nigerian National Petroleum Corporation) puts Nigeria at the 6th position of the world's top oil producers. Although this industry seems to be saturated and appears to be a monopoly of the Nigerian government, as well as the country's elite, there is still a good possibility to invest and make your own mega bucks.

The Oil and Gas industry comprises of the Upstream Sector and the Downstream sector. Multinational companies and institutional investors with expert knowledge and finance operate within this sector. Their primary activities include exploration and refining of petroleum products.

The Downstream sector is mostly driven by local entrepreneurs and businesses that engage in activities such as haulage, trucking, and sales of petroleum products, to mention a few. The industry offers lucrative investment opportunities for you to invest depending on your interest and ability to engage in the space. Some of the investment opportunities includes; Oil refinery, Fuel importation, Oil servicing, Petrol filling station, Petroleum haulage, Diesel supply and Kerosene business.

Nigeria's Infrastructure

Infrastructure plays a major role in the ability of a country to thrive, but Nigeria, so far, has not been able to keep up with the demand of its large and growing population. Of the 120,546 miles road network in Nigeria, a large portion of it is damaged or impassable.

In 2015 it had been estimated that up to \$67bn (N10.63tn) would be needed to rebuild schools, hospitals, along with bridges and roads. So here is an opportunity for investment.

The Power Sector

Electricity is another concern in Nigeria. Although statistics indicate that 45% of Nigerians are hooked to the national power grid, according to World Bank, 90 million residents are still living without electricity supply.

The national power grid is controlled by the government of Nigeria. However, entrepreneurs can invest in alternative energy sources to help Nigerians achieve their energy needs, with the government still involved through the Nigerian Electricity Regulatory Commission (NERC). This also covers alternative energy sources, so it might be worth investigating a little further.

With a total energy consumption of 1,259 TWh per annum (8.1mw per head), the need for adequate energy access is rising beyond the level sustainable by the current power grid. In the next twenty years, Nigeria is projected to need 135GW capacity to supply 230 million Nigerians. With opportunities in the generation, transmission and distribution fields, investors have no shortage of paths to take in the power sector.

Agriculture and Agro-Allied Services

Agriculture and agro-allied services are needed to help Nigerians cultivate the 80 million hectares (approximately 200 million acres) of arable land in the country. According to the IFPRI (International Food Policy Research Institute) Nigeria is not living up to its agricultural potential. Production is slow and does not promise great results, with the current level of technology and funding. But with increased investment and capital formation, more intense and reliable production can be achieved.

Investment in Agricultural commodities

Cassava has emerged as commodity number one to invest in, for estimated gross returns. The next ranked commodities are: yam, maize, millet, groundnut, rice, sorghum, poultry, leafy vegetables, and cowpea.

Other agricultural products also worth investment are: peppers, livestock, oil palm, fish, melon, tomato, soybean, onion, rubber, and cocoa.

Agribusiness Services and Products

Other than engaging in practical agricultural activities, an investor can choose to support agribusinesses with services and products such as specialized financial institutions, infrastructure provisions, fertilizer plants, tractor assembly plants, seed production research and development, warehousing services, processing plants, private insurance companies, and haulage companies.

Regulatory Services

Regulatory services such as communications, customs, and insurance are handled almost primarily by parliament, but it is a sector to look into if you have ideas that will benefit the government of Nigeria as well as its people. However, before taking on such a task, it may be wise to contact a consulting firm with experience in supporting and providing solutions to entrepreneurs.

The Security Sector

Security is a sector that requires increased spending to safeguard lives and properties. With the emergence of Boko Haram in Nigeria, in 2003, the sector is in even greater need of investment.

Security agencies are in short supply, but great demand, to help control the tide of violence by training and employing more security forces. Police are outnumbered in Nigeria, with only 371,800 policemen, at a ratio between police and citizens of 1 to 511. The development of new security firms would help decrease this ratio by training unemployed youths in the apprehension of criminals, and maintaining peace and order.

Fixed Value Chains

Infrastructure provisions such as investment in power, rural telecommunications, and irrigation projects are necessary to build a better foundation for a stable agricultural system in Nigeria. Private insurance companies are needed to provide weather-based insurance services and specialized financial institutions are needed to lend to fixed value chains. With these established, the Nigerian agricultural services sector will be more adept at generating income from the natural resources of the land.

The Automotive Sector

This sector is very important to the NIRP (Nigerian Industrial Revolution Plan). The NIRP is a program put in place by the Ministry of Industry, Trade and Investments, for a period of 5 years, to help establish diversification of the country's economy and revenue, and to increase manufacturing industry contribution to the GDP.

With its present installed auto capacity, great labor force, important local demand, and strategic location for export, Nigeria is well positioned and qualified to be a major Assembly Hub for the International Auto companies

Studies by the Financial Vanguard reported that, Nigeria spent a total of N1.2 trillion on vehicles importation only in the year 2013. A breakdown of the figure showed N550 billion spent on importation of cars, buses and trucks, N500 billion on spare parts, and on tyres alone, N150 billion.

This report specified that the benefitting companies are automobile manufacturing giants such as Toyota, Honda, General Appliances West Africa, Perfection Motors Company, and Richbon Nigeria. But also R.T. Briscoe Nigeria, Nigeria-China Manufacturing Company, Nigeria Sino Trucks, Coacharis

Motors, DAG Motorcycle Industry Nigeria, Globe Motors Nigeria, Century Auto-Assembly Nigeria, and Concept Auto Centre.

It's projected that the plants will produce a wide range of automobile products, such as sport utility vehicles, passenger cars, pickup vans, buses, tricycles and motorcycles.

Information and Communication Technology (ICT)

The city of Lagos in Nigeria, dubbed: Africa's Silicon Valley by some, has a huge population, and a mobile penetration of approximately 75% translating into 130 million mobiles. Nigeria is well on its way to marking itself a hotspot for tech start-ups in the whole continent. It is the largest mobile market in Africa and the 24th biggest economy in the world.

Today in Nigeria, an explosion in E Commerce has been experienced, with companies such as: Jumia Nigeria, Konga, Dealdey, Yudala, Payporte, Vconnect, Kara and many more. People shop online more than ever before. The most prominent sectors are: Fashion, Groceries and food, Delivery and logistics, Real estate, Furniture, Electronics, Travel and Automobile.

There is a substantial untapped potential in every niche for tech start-ups. Bigger opportunities lie in finance, E commerce, agriculture and education. For people eager to meet the needs of these sectors through technology, the required support could be attained from start-up accelerator programs, the many venture capitalists and angel investors installed in Nigeria.

CHAPTER 3
FRANCHISE OPPORTUNITIES

Franchise Opportunities in Nigeria

Multiple sectors of the Nigerian economy are open to franchising. These opportunities have massively increased in the past few years, and translate to market growth opportunities for foreign companies interested in bringing their brands and market into Nigeria. This form of business creates opportunities with the advantages of low cost advertisement and high returns on investment. Coupled with technical support from the mother company (franchisor), it is a win-win situation when done correctly and intelligently.

Franchises Present in Nigeria

Some International companies:

- Kentucky Fried Chicken,
- Domino's Pizza,
- Subway,
- Crestcom International,
- Bird's Eye Global Tracking,
- Snap Fitness
- BCM and many more

    Some Local companies:

- Dream Cones,
- Chicken Republic,
- Mr. Biggs,
- Tantalizers
- Century 21 Nigeria
- Modern Montossori International and many more

How to Set Up a Franchise in Nigeria

To setup a franchise, a specified amount of money to buy or start the franchise will be required. The amount required varies from one franchising company to another. Going by the standard, here is what to expect from the Franchisors; the franchisee shall be allowed to use the franchisor's established brand and products and will also get support services from the franchisor's support unit. To access this privilege, the franchisee shall pay a one-time franchise fee and will remit a portion of the profits to the franchising company.

To make sure you are going for the right franchisor, it is recommended that you carry out in-depth research, keeping in mind your budget for investment, management skills, and personal abilities.

In order to get additional information on franchising in Nigeria, readable materials have been made available by the Nigerian International Franchise Association (nigerianfranchise.org) and the International Franchise Association.

CHAPTER 4
START-UP OPPORTUNITIES

Why set up your Start-up in Nigeria?

Reports presented by the United Nations (UN) and United Nations Development Program (UNDP) on Nigeria, suggest that the country is the sixth most populous nation in the world after China, India, US, Indonesia and Brazil. Nigeria's population growth rate was estimated (average annual percentage) at 2.5% from 2010 to 2015; its urban growth rate from 2010 to 2015 was estimated at 3.8%; its rural population growth rate from 2010 to 2015 at 1.3%; Nigeria's urban population in 2012 was 50.3%; As for the primary-secondary school's enrolment ratios for male and female per 100 persons in 2012, we had 62.0% and 68.9% respectively. The Internet usage was estimated at 46.1% in the year 2016; and the literacy rate at 39% – 51%.

So, when thinking of setting up a business, the possibilities in Nigeria are endless. There are opportunities across the different sectors with potential for high success rate.

Having considered all these facts, in order for your Start-up to become a success story, here are some steps to help you plan, manage, and prepare your business for success in Nigeria.

Your Business Idea

Your first step will of course be, your business idea. Figure out what you want to do, what needs to be done to accomplish it, and if you have the capacity to put in the work it will require. The idea could be a business that solves a problem, or it could simply be an innovative product or service that you will introduce to the market.

Your Business Plan

Although quite a few successful entrepreneurs debate the importance of a business plan, developing on could still be of great help at the early stages. With a well-thought-out business plan, the goals and objectives of a business are clearly stated and can serve as reference point at any given time in the business life. It's important to keep in mind that the initial business plan may not be the ultimate plan. Here are a few benefits and reasons for a Business Plan:

- **Strategy reminder.** Your business plan will summarize the main points of your strategy.

- **Clear business objectives.** You can use your plan to define and manage specific objectives, as well as identifying your potential market, sales, cost of sales, lead processing, business processing etc.

- **Clarity on interdependencies.** Keep track of what needs to be done and in what order.

- **Tracking through Milestones.** It can also be used to keep track of dates and deadlines.

- **Delegating.** The business plan will clarify who is responsible for what.

- **Manage cash flow.** A cash flow plan will help put together all your forecast on sales, costs, expenses, assets and debts.

Your Team

Creating a Start-up is a massive job that might require the entrepreneur to juggle quite a few roles. That being said, not many people have the skill set for every role and trying to take on too many, could be detrimental to your company. So as much as you might have to take on a few responsibilities, especially at the start of your business, building a team and the right team must be part of your immediate plans. So, once you've had an honest conversation about what skills you lack, find people who believe in your idea and have the skills you require.

Your Business Location

The old saying is true for businesses in Nigeria, as it is in the rest of the world: it's all about "location, location, location!" The location you choose for your business should be around your target market ideally. When looking for business sites, make sure it isn't in a spot that is hard to reach or secluded. The best location for your business should be easily located and accessible.

Your Capital

The first 4 steps are crucial, for anyone planning to build a successful business but when it comes to capital requirements, it depends on the business type. Some service oriented businesses or IT savvy ventures might not necessarily require financial capital but will require human capital to kick-start the business. However, for most businesses, you will need finances to start, scale, and grow your business (purchase assets and maintain operations).

There are different ways one could raise capital for a start-up:

- Get or stay in a job and save up, whilst planning and working on the business

- Look for an angel investor who would believe in the idea and fund it

- Start a little side business from which you can save up

- Ask family and friends for little amounts, which could ultimately amount to the required capital

- Or simply partner with someone who will put in the funds

It is not advisable to start a business with a loan.

Your Registration with the Government

You will be required to register your business with the government. The Article of Association could be a useful tool, as it contains a lot of information on businesses in Nigeria. To register a limited liability company (LLC), you might need to employ the services of a business law lawyer or a consultancy agency. If registering a business is not an option, then you might consider registering a business name to kick-start your operations.

Your Registration with the Federal and State Tax Offices

You will also be required to register with the federal and state tax offices. When you register with the Federal Inland Revenue Service (FIRS), you will be provided with your Tax Identification Number (TIN), which will be needed to open a business bank account and carrying out tax clearance.

Your Business Bank Account

After successfully raising capital, registering your business with the government, registering with the Federal and State Tax offices, and acquiring your TIN, the next step is to set up a business bank account in which the business start-up capital will be deposited.

This account will be used solely for business transactions such as paying bills, receiving monies from customers in exchange for goods or services, and paying employees. However, you might not require this if you choose to operate as a sole trader with a mere business name.

CHAPTER 5

STEP-BY-STEP HOW TO REGISTER YOUR BUSINESS

Incorporation v. Registration

Registering a business in Nigeria can be achieved by incorporation of a company or registering a business name. A foreign company may be exempted from registration if it belongs to one of the following categories:

- Foreign companies invited to Nigeria by, or with the approval of, the Federal Government, to execute any specified individual project;

- Foreign companies which are in Nigeria for the execution of specific individual loan on behalf of a donor country or international organization;

- Foreign government-owned companies engaged solely in export promotion activities;

- Engineering consultants and technical experts on any individual specialist project under contract with any of the governments or any of their agencies or with any other body or person, where such contract has been approved by the Federal Government.

How to Register a Business (CAC)

The Corporate Affairs Commission (CAC) is the governmental body responsible for registering business names and companies in Nigeria. The registration of companies in Nigeria can take an average of 28 days. You could choose to register a business in Nigeria as any of the following:

- Private Limited Liability Company;

- Public Limited Liability Company;

- Unlimited Liability Company;

- Company Limited by Guarantee;

- Foreign Company (branch or subsidiary of foreign company);

- Partnership/Firm;

- Sole Proprietorship;

- Incorporated trustees (religious, charitable, philanthropic, or cultural); and

13

- Representative office (in special cases)

CAC Registration Steps

Registration of all companies is handled by the Corporate Affairs Commission (CAC). Here are the different steps:

- Name reservation at CAC: 5 days

- Incorporation documents and stamp duty: 7 days

- Declaration of compliance: 1 day

- Registration and fees at CAC: 11 days

- Income tax and VAT at FIRS: 4 days

- Personal income tax and PAYE at state tax office: 2 days

- Registration of location and paying premises levy: 1 day

Filling Out the CAC Form

If your company is not exempt from registration, the next step will be to complete the registration by filing the necessary CAC form. However, prior to filling out form, the CAC requires that you choose two to three unique names for your company. This will entail you doing a name search, using the Availability Form from CAC, at a price of N500 (Five Hundred Naira) subject to increase (Could be more if using a lawyer), then choose two to three unique names for your company.

If one of the names you chose is found fitting and unregistered, it will be allocated to you and reserved for 60 days.

CAC Form Requirements

You will have to fill in:

- The Company's name,

- The full names, ages, and residential addresses of all the directors

- The company's address (Which must be within Nigeria),

- The company's Share Capital (Must be stated on the form marked CAC 2),

- The name of the company secretary must also be included.

Additional Documents

Along with the CAC form, you'll have to provide:

- Means of identification for all the members of the company with a certificate of proficiency.

- The memorandum and articles of association, which traditionally form the constitution of the company. The memorandum sets out the structure and conditions of the company while articles contain the special regulations for the internal management of affairs of the company as long as they are provided in the Act.

- The notice of the address of the registered office must also be provided, and the notice must state the address of the registered office and the head office of the company. This must be a physical address; a post office box or private mail bag is not acceptable.

- List particulars and consent of the first director – a statement in a prescribed form containing the list and particulars together with the consent of the persons who are to be the first directors of the company – will also need to be filed.

- The statement of the authorized share capital, which must show the authorized share capital divided into shares of a fixed amount e.g. N10,000 divided into 10,000 shares of N1 each and must be signed by a director.

- The Commission's form for consent to the use of the proposed name.

- And a business and resident permit in the case of foreigner who is proposed as a director, secretary or subscriber to the memorandum.

CORPORATE AFFAIRS COMMISSION

FORM CAC 1A

CHANGE OF NAME AVAILABILITY CHECK AND RESERVATION OF NAME
Pursuant to Sections 31, 662 and 676

Name of Presenter:					
Accreditation No:			Telephone No.:		
Address:					
			City		
State		P.O. Box		Email	

RC. NO.:

NAME OF COMPANY/BUSINESS NAME/INCORPORATED TRUSTEES

PROPOSED NAME OF COMPANY/BUSINESS/INCORPORATED TRUSTEES:

OPTION ONE

OPTION TWO

The name is to be used for:

a. Private Limited Company (LTD) ☐   d. Company Limited By Guarantee (LTD/GTE) ☐

b. Public Limited Company (PLC) ☐   e. Business Name ☐

c. Unlimited Company (ULTD) ☐   f. Incorporated Trustees ☐

Dated this _____ **Day of** _____ **20** _____

_____
Signature of Presenter

16

How to File Incorporation Documents

Once ready and properly stamped, all documents must be presented to the Commission for filing. There is a filing fee, which changes occasionally.

In addition to the filing fees, there are other registration fees payable to the Commission:

- Registration of public company having share capital;

- Registration of private company having share capital; and

- Registration of a company not having share capital.

Once the requirements of the law have been complied with, and the documents have been introduced to the commission, a statutory declaration in a prescribed form must be drafted by a legal practitioner, stating the requirements for registration have been duly completed. You will then receive a Certificates of Incorporation.

NIPC Registration

The NIPC (Nigerian Investment Promotion Commission) is a Federal Government Agency in Nigeria established by the NIPC Act N0. 16 of 1995 to promote, co-ordinate and monitor all investments in Nigeria. Here is the procedure to register with the NIPC:

- Fill the NIPC Form1 (It can be downloaded online from the NIPC website: www.nipc.gov.ng),

- Pay a non-refundable deposit of N10,000.00 and make sure you receive and keep a receipt. NIPC Form1

- Provide two copies of your receipt for payment of N10,000.00,

- Your Certificate of Incorporation,

- The memorandum and Articles of Association of the company,

- Receipts for payment of stamp duties on the authorized share capital of the company at the date of application,

- Tax clearance certificate of the applicant company,

- Partnership or joint-venture agreement where applicable,

- Feasibility report and project implementation program of the company for its proposed business,

- Title deeds of land evidencing firm commitment to acquire requisite business premises for the company's operations,

- Training program for the Nigerian staff or personnel policy of the company, incorporating management succession schedule for qualified Nigerians,

- Names, addresses, nationalities, and occupations of the proposed directors of the company, (including non-resident directors, which should be marked NRD),

- Job title designations of expatriate quota positions required, and the academic and working experience required for the occupations of such positions,

- Information brochure, if any, on the foreign partner, and

- Evidence of capital importation for wholly foreign companies.

Following the above step by step process, should assist you in successfully registering your business in The Federal Republic of Nigeria. The process may seem a little long winded, but once achieved it becomes more rewarding with the knowledge that your business idea has become a registered and recognized organization by the CAC in Nigeria.

CHAPTER 6
LAWS AND REGULATIONS

Nigeria, just as any other nation, has a number of laws governing business relations within its borders. Knowledge and understanding of these laws and regulations is a necessary part of starting a business in Nigeria and should not be ignored or disregarded.

The closer you follow the laws and regulations set forth by the Nigerian government, the more likely your business is to survive and thrive. The following section details the most important laws and regulations for investors and entrepreneurs wishing to set up a business.

Laws

The Immigration Act

No person other than a citizen of Nigeria shall set up a business or participate in a trade or business in the form of a partnership without the consent in writing of the Director of Immigration. A foreigner is required to obtain four basic permits before he can set up or participate in any business in Nigeria:

- Entry permit or visa,

- Expatriate quota,

- Business permit, and

- Residence permit

As a matter of first importance to operate any business in Nigeria, it must be enlisted with the Corporate Affairs Commission (CAC) be it a small, medium, or large corporations. The CAC is the autonomous body in charge of regulating the formation and management of organizations in Nigeria.

Nigerian Investment Promotion Commission (NIPC) Act, Cap NI17 LFN 2004

Section 17 of the Nigerian Investment Promotion Commission Act states that any non-Nigerian can make an investment in Nigeria, but will require an alien to register with the Commission before commencing business.

Foreign Exchange (Monitoring and Miscellaneous Provisions) Act

The "FEM Act" is an act to establish an Autonomous Foreign Exchange Market, to provide for the monitoring and supervision of the transactions conducted in the market, and for matters connected therewith.

FEM Act, Cap F.34 LFN 2004

This section of the act refers to jurisdiction of the Autonomous Foreign Exchange Market.

The National Office for Technology Acquisition and Promotion Act

This act states that all foreign companies interested in transferring foreign technology into Nigeria, will have to register all the documents or agreements involving the transfer of foreign technology with the National Office for Technology Acquisition Commission.

A contract or agreement involves transfer of technology if it includes:

- The use of trademarks,

- The right to use patented inventions,

- The supply of technical expertise in the form of the preparation of plans, diagrams, operating manuals, or any other form of technical assistance of any description whatsoever,

- The supply of basic or detailed engineering,

- The supply of machinery and plant engineering,

- The provision of operating staff or managerial assistance and the training of personnel.

This application must be done no later than 60 days from the execution or completion of the contract, and addressed to the director of the National Office for Technology Acquisition and Promotion, along with all the certified true copies of such contract and agreement, as well as all other related documents and information.

Cap N. 62 LFN 2004

This act establishes a body (NOTAP) to monitor the transfer of foreign technology to Nigeria and provides for related matters.

Companies and Allied Matters (CAMA) Act, Cap. C. 20 LFN 2004

This act states that a foreign company wishing to carry on business in Nigeria must be incorporated under CAMA before carrying on business in Nigeria.

Investments and Securities Act (ISA) 2007

Section 8 of the Investments and Securities Act, empowers the Securities and Exchange Commission (SEC) to keep and maintain Foreign Direct Investments (FDI) and Foreign Portfolio Investments (FPI) in Nigeria.

Industrial Inspectorate Act, Cap. I 8 LFN 2004

This act was established for the purpose of investigation of industries involved in investments and related activities.

The Nigerian Investment Promotion Commission Act 1995

The NIPC Act is one of the most important laws to know when starting a business in Nigeria. The Nigerian Investment Promotion Commission (NIPC) Act No.16 of 1995 has abolished any restrictions, in respect of the limits of foreign shareholding, in Nigeria registered/domiciled enterprises.

Required Personnel

The Companies and Allied Matters Act of 2004 demands that all companies in Nigeria have at least two directors. Consequently, you need to have your directors by the time you are filling the incorporation forms, as well as a company secretary.

Also, you will need to have a minimum of two people, enlisted as members of the company. A member of the company is the body of persons that make up the company. For a private company, a minimum of two and maximum of 50 members are required.

A minors (below the age of 18) can be enlisted as a director in a company provided there are two other adults listed as directors.

Exemptions

There are some businesses that are exempted from free and unrestrained contribution, irrespective of their nationality. These are:

- Production of arms and ammunition;

- Production of and dealing in narcotic drugs and psychotropic substances;

- Manufacture of military/paramilitary wears and accoutrements; and

-    Participation in coastal and inland shipping.

Regulations

Regulatory Bodies in Nigeria

Other factors to consider are the relevant regulatory bodies a business may be bound to. A regulatory body or agency, also known as a regulator, is a public authority or government agency responsible for exercising autonomous authority over some area of human activity in a regulatory or supervisory capacity.

The regulatory agencies enforce rules and regulations and impose supervision, in the area of administrative law regulation. All investors must register with the necessary and relevant regulatory bodies.

Know the Relevant Regulatory Bodies

There are many regulatory bodies in Nigeria supervising different sectors in the Nigerian economy. Some of those regulatory bodies are:

-    The Financial sector: Central Bank of Nigeria, Nigeria Deposit Insurance Corporation, Security and Exchange Commission, National Insurance Commission (NAICOM), Federal Inland Revenue Service (FIRS),

-    The Telecommunication sector: Nigerian Communications Commission

-    The oil sector: Ministry of Petroleum Resources (MPR), Department of Petroleum Resources (DPR), Nigerian National Petroleum Corporation (NNPC), Federal Inland Revenue Service (FIRS).

Business Taxation Standards

In Nigeria, a company's income tax rate is 30% with an additional education tax of 2%. Approximately 5% withholding tax is chargeable on unearned income. For foreign investors, the 10% withholding tax on individuals is the final tax on dividends. As for personal income tax rate it is calculated at 5%.

The Capital Gains Tax rate is 10%. Shares in companies are exempt from capital gains tax, which is a very significant tax relief for investors. Stamp duty is chargeable for various documents. There are pay-as-you-earn income tax regulations, and various social insurance type contributions that are compulsory.

Expatriate Quota

Expatriate quota positions are usually granted for two to three years and are subject to renewal, except in cases where companies qualify for and are granted PUR quota (Permanent Until Reviewed). The advantage local companies have over foreign establishments is that they have access to funds, grants, and more from the government, CBN, and institutions such as Bank of Industry (BOI) and Bank of Agriculture (BOA). The advantage foreign organizations have is their pioneer status.

Pioneer Status

A number of industries are declared "pioneer industries", by the Industrial Development (Income Tax Relief) Act, Cap. 179 Laws of Nigeria, 1990. This comes in place when, the activities of a company include the production of pioneer and non-pioneer products. This will then activate a company relief from income tax liability for a period of up to five years. In order to qualify for the Pioneer Status, the amount of qualifying capital investment in the business must be verifiable by physical inspection, supported by a report by the Industrial Inspectorate Division of the Federal Ministry of Industry before a Pioneer Certificate is granted.

Foreign Direct Investment

Foreign Direct Investment (FDI) is a measure of foreign ownership of productive assets, such as factories, mines, and land. An expatriate could register a business name as a sole proprietor (or partnership) subject to a business permit, or can incorporate a company with other foreigners or with Nigerians. Where incorporating a company, they may do business in all sectors, but the areas included in what is called, the negative list (arms and ammunition; narcotic drugs and psychotropic substances; para-military and military wears and accoutrement).

CHAPTER 7

TIPS AND ADVICE

The continent of Africa is an explosion of diversity, not only from one nation to another but also within each country. Nigeria is a perfect example of this diversity. Therefore, before going into business in Nigeria, it is important to be well prepared.

Checklist questionnaire:

- What type of business (and in what industry) are you hoping to invest?

- What is your target market audience?

- What size company?

- Will you be handling the business on site or from abroad?

- Will your business require employees?

- Will your business require a physical location/venue?

- Are you creating this business as a foreigner or as a citizen of the country?

- Are you familiar with the country?

- Is your business a new concept that will need to be introduced to the people?

- Will you be running the day-to-day activities of the business?

- Do you have help/contacts in your country of choice?

- Do you know how much capital will be required to start off?

- What is your capital?

Advise and recommendations:

You can be sure that your idea or business will be successful if you put in the work required:

- Understand who your target audience/market is.

- Locate the area of the country best suited to accommodate your business.

- Connect with people who could be of help.

- Choose the right publicity channels to make yourself and your business known.

- Also, going in with a partner can save you a lot of money and cut the workload considerably. Remember, you don't have to stay in a partnership forever, but it is an easier and quicker way to get started.

- Choose your investment sector: The financial sector has different rules from the educational sector, for example, and this will impact the way you set up your business.

- Develop a detailed business plan: It must lay out your specific goals and be sure that they are realistic. While passion and ambition are essential, you must also have specific business objectives and a clear vision as to how to meet those goals.

- Be competent and coherent when it comes to today's technology and processes: This is a vital step, even if your product is not in the high tech or digital field. Some of the means for marketing your products or running your business will be digital, so you need to understand software and digital processes. You must be technologically literate, in order to compete in today's market. Customers will expect no less.

- Know your clients: Make it a point to know as much as possible about your clients and potential clients. Your customers are your business. Without them there is no business. Know and treat them well. Find the best means of communication with your customers.

- Know what you need: You might consider engaging locally hired representatives to provide guidance on the business environment, identify customers, and obtain market information. For products requiring after-sales service and spare parts, it is recommended that exporters consider operating through a distributor or dealership. Agents and distributors must register with the government and their contracts must be notarized and published in the local press.

Attention

Just as in any other country in the world, corruption does exist in Nigeria. It is advised to go through the right channels and institutions whilst creating your business.

Should you decide to travel to Nigeria, be aware of all the visa requirements. Travelers should obtain the latest information on entry requirements from the nearest Nigerian embassy or consulate.

Last Considerations for Business Strategy in Nigeria

Constantly research on market trends and best practices, to improve on your services and deliverables, then update your business plans to compete with contemporary competitors. Growth – not only geographically, but intellectually and technologically – is the single most important aspect all successful businesses have in common.

Also, foreign companies are not obliged to be registered in Nigeria, so long as a letter is written to the secretary for the Federal state. Consequently, foreign nationals enjoy the fact that the taxation that they have to pay in case their companies are registered in the country is not discriminative and they pay just like the rest of the citizens.

Companies with foreign participation are required to register with the NIPC on incorporation and obtain a business permit prior to commencement of business. A minimum share capital of N10,000,000.00 is required for companies applying for a Nigerian Business Permit. Employment of non-Nigerians is subject to an Expatriate Quota Approval, which can be issued by the NIPC. Foreign companies aiming to invest in the hydrocarbon sector will have to obtain an additional permit from the Department of Petroleum Resources (DPR), the regulatory body responsible for oil & gas matters in Nigeria.

Finally

Setting up a business in Nigeria can be done with relative ease for someone who is driven, pays close attention to detail and knows all there is to know on his business and portion of the market (Do your homework and research diligently). It is not an undertaking that should be entered into lightly, given that it takes time, patience, and commitment to become successful in a market that is open and ready to receive new investors and entrepreneurs.

Resources for Further Research

The organizations and resources listed below were used as reference or have been partially introduced in this book. Should you need more information or require help to start your business in South Africa or any other African country, please contact us via our website: www.startabusinessinafrica.com, email: info@startabusinessinafrica.com or social media @SABIAFRICA1 and we will be more than happy to assist.

1. ABOKFIX: Your Daily Naira Exchange Rate. http://abokifx.com/

2. Africa Check: Explaining Nigeria's Boko Haram and its violent insurgency. https://africacheck.org/factsheets/factsheet-explaining-nigerias-boko-haram-and-its-violent-insurgency/

3. African Development Bank Group: Nigeria Economic Outlook. http://www.afdb.org/en/countries/west-africa/nigeria/nigeria-economic-outlook/

4. All Africa: Vanguard: Nigeria: History, Structure of the Roads System. http://allafrica.com/stories/200806240144.html

5. American Embassy in Nigeria: United States Diplomatic Mission to Nigeria. http://nigeria.usembassy.gov/

6. Bank of Agriculture, Nigeria: http://www.boanig.com/

7. Bank of Industry, Nigeria: http://www.boi.ng/

8. Central Bank of Nigeria: The Foreign Exchange Market in Nigeria. https://www.cbn.gov.ng/IntOps/FXMarket.asp

9. Corporate Affairs Commission: http://new.cac.gov.ng/home/

10. Department of Petroleum Resources: https://dpr.gov.ng/index/

11. The Economist: Nigeria has about as much electricity as Edinburgh. That is a problem. http://www.economist.com/news/middle-east-and-africa/21693971-nigeria-has-about-much-electricity-edinburgh-problem-powerless

12. Federal Inland Revenue Service: https://recruitment.firs.gov.ng/

13. Federal Ministry of Industry, Trade, and Investment: http://www.fmiti.gov.ng/

14. International Franchise Association: http://www.franchise.org/nigeria

15. Investopedia: What is a 'Foreign Direct Investment - FDI'? http://www.investopedia.com/terms/f/fdi.asp

16. Joci Entertainment World: INDUSTRIAL INSPECTORATE ACT CAP. 180 L.F.N. 1990 ACT CAP I8 L.F.N. 2004. https://jewngr.files.wordpress.com/2013/05/industrial-inspectorate-act.pdf

17. Law Nigeria: Foreign Exchange Monitoring and Miscellaneous Provisions Act. http://lawnigeria.com/LawsoftheFederation/FOREIGN-EXCHANGE-%28MONITORING-AND-MISCELLANEOUS-PROVISIONS%29-ACT.html

18. Ministry of Petroleum: http://petroleumresources.gov.ng/

19. NAIJ: A look at Mandilas Market in Lagos. https://www.naij.com/775607-a-look-at-mandilas-market-in-lagos.html

20. Naira Land: Requirements For Expatriate Quota and Business permit In Nigeria. http://www.nairaland.com/1522846/requirements-expatriate-quota-business-permit

21. National Insurance Commission: http://naicom.gov.ng/

22. National Office for Technology Acquisition and Promotion: http://www.notap.gov.ng/

23. Nigeria Deposit Insurance Corporation: http://ndic.gov.ng/

24. Nigeria Exports Processing Zones Authority: Nigeria Industrial Revolution Plan. http://www.nepza.gov.ng/downloads/nirp.pdf

25. Nigeria Investment Promotion Commission: http://www.nipc.gov.ng/

26. Nigeria Law: http://www.nigeria-law.org

27. Nigerian Communications Commission: http://www.ncc.gov.ng/

28. Nigerian International Franchise Association: http://www.nigerianfranchise.org/

29. Nigerian Law Intellectual Property Watch: National Office for Technology Acquisition and Promotion Act (NOTAP Act). http://nlipw.com/national-office-for-technology-acquisition-and-promotion-act/

30. Nigerian National Petroleum Corporation: http://www.nnpcgroup.com/

31. Observe Nigeria: The Largest IT Market in Nigeria, Computer Village Lagos. https://www.observenigeria.com/cultures/largest-i-t-market-nigeria-computer-village-lagos/

32. Securities and Exchange Commission: http://sec.gov.ng/

33. Supporting Economic Transformation in Nigeria: Supporting Economic Transformation in Nigeria, May 2016. http://set.odi.org/wp-content/uploads/2016/05/SET-Nigeria-Paper-May-2016.pdf

34. U.S. Small Business Administration: Write Your Business Plan. https://www.sba.gov/starting-business/write-your-business-plan

35. Vanguard: Naira slides against Dollar as Nigeria surrenders title as largest economy in Africa. http://www.vanguardngr.com/2016/08/naira-slides-dollar-nigeria-surrenders-title-largest-economy-africa/

www.ingramcontent.com/pod-product-compliance
Lightning Source LLC
Chambersburg PA
CBHW031506210526
45463CB00003B/1105